MY LIFE LESSONS ON LIVING A LIFE YOU LOVE

The Little Book About
YOU ARE DEFINITELY MORE THAN YOU THINK YOU ARE

Dieter Langenecker

Modern Elder

Humanistic Counselor (Meaning, Wisdom, Soul)

Copyright © 2024 Dieter Langenecker

ALL RIGHTS RESERVED. No part of this book may be reproduced or transmitted in any form or by any means, electronic or mechanical, including photocopying, recording, video, or by any information and retrieval system, without prior written permission from the publisher. The scanning, uploading, and distribution of this book via the Internet or via any other means without the prior written permission of the publisher is illegal and punishable by law.

Published via Amazon KDP (Kindle Direct Publishing)

ISBN 9798340031938

Disclaimer:
The content, grammar, and spelling of this book were reviewed and refined with the assistance of friends and AI.

Please Note:

(NN) stands for "Nomen Nescio" (Latin), which means the author's name of the quote is unknown.

Veronica, Yolanda, Victor, Fau, Romeo,

Yoli, Cristina, and Jimena

You've unlocked a new depth of fulfillment in my life

Thank you!

Let me express my heartfelt gratitude to everyone I've encountered throughout my life. Your direct and indirect feedback has been invaluable in helping me find greater inner peace, cultivate compassion, and live a life I truly love. Thank you for being part of this meaningful path.

Contents

Contents	1
Introduction	3
1. Forget Happiness	5
What is Happiness?	9
The Last Freedom	13
From Having to Doing to Being	17
2. Inner Peace, Calm, and Strength	19
Know Yourself, really!	23
Inner Meaning	27
3. Being	29
How real is reality?	33
Spirituality, Non-Duality, and Quantum Mechanics	37
Coming Home	41
Nature	45
My Trick	49
Brushing Your Soul	53
Exercises	79
Epilogue	83
Inspiring Quotes	101
About Dieter Langenecker	

Introduction

What Is It all about?

When it is the time to die, how do you know you have lived a fulfilling life?

Life is a journey, a series of moments strung together like beads on a string. Some of these moments are filled with joy, others with pain, and many with the mundane tasks that fill our days. But beneath the surface of our daily lives lies something deeper—a call to live a life that is not just filled with things, accomplishments, or even fleeting happiness, but with true meaning, inner peace, and a sense of fulfillment that resonates in our souls.

This book is a collection of thoughts, reflections, and lessons that I have gathered over the years. It is my attempt to distill what I have learned about living a life that is truly loved—a life that goes beyond the pursuit of happiness to the pursuit of being. It is written for my family, but also for anyone who feels the pull to live more authentically, with compassion for themselves and the world around them.

Life has been a journey filled with ups and downs—each challenge offers the greatest opportunities for learning and growth. Through it all, the philosophies of Taoism, Buddhism, and Stoicism, as well as insights from Quantum Mechanics and Non-Duality, have been my companions. These teachings have guided me to travel my path with curiosity and equanimity, helping me to embrace both the highs and lows with a sense of wonder and acceptance. They've shown me that life's complexities can be navigated not with rigid answers, but with an open heart and a resilient spirit.

I'm not here to give you a strict set of rules to follow or a formula for living. Life doesn't work that way. Instead, consider these chapters as offerings on a buffet—take what resonates with you, what nourishes your soul, and leave behind what doesn't quite fit. Let these reflections serve as inspiration and encouragement as you navigate your own unique path. Be open to exploring new perspectives but trust yourself to discern what truly aligns with who you are. This is your journey, and only you can decide what it means to live a life you truly love.

As you read, I encourage you to take your time. Pause where you feel drawn, skip ahead if you wish, and return to the passages that resonate with you. This is your journey, and this book is simply a companion along the way.

In the end, my hope is that these words will inspire you to live a life you truly love—a life that is yours, and yours alone.

Vienna, December 2024   Dieter Langenecker

FORGET HAPPINESS

What is Happiness?

"I had to make you uncomfortable, otherwise you never would have moved." (Universe)

"When I was 17, I used to admire people with luxuries. Now, I admire people with inner peace." (NN)

"Happiness is not about getting all you want, it is about enjoying all there is – and this is called fulfillment." (NN)

"Maybe this new path you're being redirected to is the path you were meant to be on all along. Release your grip, surrender, love." (NN)

"My mission, should I choose to accept it, is to find peace with exactly who and what I am. To take pride in my thoughts, my appearance, my talents, my flaws, and to stop this incessant worrying that I cannot be loved as I am." (Anais Nin)

"Happiness is the absence of the striving for happiness." (Chuang-Tzu)

A big shift is happening.

Forget happiness.

Embrace fulfillment.

I challenge the notion that happiness should be our ultimate goal in life.

Society tells us that happiness lies in achieving wealth, success, and material possessions. From an early age, we're taught that reaching these milestones will bring lasting fulfillment. But in my experience, the relentless pursuit of happiness often leads to disappointment. We chase after it, only to find that it fades quickly, leaving us searching for the next thing.

Happiness is fleeting, like waves that come and go. The more we chase it, the more elusive it becomes, creating a sense of emptiness as we constantly seek the next achievement to fill the void. This cultural obsession traps us in a never-ending race, with happiness always just out of reach.

External markers of success might bring temporary joy, but they often feel hollow, disconnected from our true selves. True fulfillment, I've learned, doesn't come from these external achievements. Instead, it's found in cultivating inner resources and discovering contentment beyond material possessions.

To find genuine fulfillment, I've had to shift my perspective—happiness is a momentary emotion, but contentment is deeper and more sustainable. It embraces the full range of life's experiences and focuses on inner peace, strength, and meaningful compassion—for oneself and the world around us.

After all, you are more than you think you are.

The Last Freedom

"Everything can be taken from a man but one thing: the last of the human freedoms—to choose one's attitude in any given set of circumstances." (Viktor Frankl)

"Success can fill your bank account, but not your soul." (NN)

"I'm ready for a new chapter in my life." (NN)

"A 'fresh start' isn't a new place, it's a mindset." (NN)

"We all have "issues" because we all have a story. And no matter how much work you have done on yourself, we all snap back sometimes. So be easy on yourself. Development is a dance. Not a light switch." (NN)

In the 1970s, I attended a speech by Dr. Viktor Frankl, the psychiatrist and author of *Man's Search for Meaning*, who spent three years in Nazi concentration camps. He was addressing a group of young entrepreneurs in Vienna, using nothing more than a blackboard and chalk.

Frankl drew a horizontal line on the blackboard, labeling one end "failure" and the other "success". He explained that much of our lives are spent striving for success, which is primarily defined by external measures—how much money we make, our rank in a company, and the respect we receive from our peers. Success often involves being measured against others.

Failure	Success
0%	100%

Frankl believed there is a separate dimension that is often overlooked in our thinking and planning but is critical to our well-being. He drew a vertical line across the horizontal one, calling it the "fulfillment- depression" line. Fulfillment, he explained, is the deeply felt sense that your life is full, whole, and complete—that you have expanded to "fill up" your potential. Unlike success, fulfillment is largely defined by internal measures, by how we feel about what we are doing or have done.

```
                    Fulfilment
                        |
                        |
         III            |           I
                        |
  Failure               |                Success
  ─────────────────────────────────────────────
  0%                    |                100%
                        |
         IV             |           II
                        |
                        |
                    Depression
```

The goal, Frankl noted, is to find yourself in quadrant I—where fulfillment and success intersect. Naturally, we all want to avoid quadrant IV. As an example of quadrant III—outer failure but inner fulfillment—Frankl mentioned the monks in the Himalayan Mountains. He emphasized that this is not our culture and not something to imitate, but rather a different way of living.

The sad reality, he added, is that in our culture, many people find themselves in quadrant II—outer success but inner depression. To compensate for their depression, they often try even harder to achieve more "success", instead of focusing on their fulfillment.

From Having to Doing to Being

"It is only with the heart that one can see rightly; what is essential is invisible to the eye." (Antoine de Saint-Exupéry)

"Stop waiting for Friday, for someone to fall in love with, for life. Fulfillment is achieved when you make the most of the moment you are in now." (NN)

"If your 'happiness' depends upon what is happening outside of you, you are a slave to the external situation." (Sadhguru)

" 'We only live once, Snoopy' – 'Wrong! We only die once. We live every day!' " (Snoopy and friends, Charles Schultz)

"The older you get, the more you realize that it is okay to live a life others do not understand." (NN)

What Is Fulfillment?

In my view, there are three key areas in life: Having, Doing, and Being.

Having is where we believe that accumulating "stuff" (or relationships) will make us happy.

Doing is where we think that by engaging in activities—preferably meaningful ones—we will find happiness.

Being is simply existing in the present moment. This means not being driven by emotional wounds from the past, not feeling compelled to meet others' expectations (or our own) in the present, and not being ruled by the fear of the future or the unknown.

Let's be honest: we may never fully achieve this state of pure Being, but shouldn't we strive to get as close to it as possible?

Ultimately, fulfillment lies in finding a balance between these three areas. We should aim to have only what we truly need, avoid falling into the trap of meaningless busyness, and focus on being present and enjoying the now as much as we can.

After all, we are Human Beings, not Human Doings or Human Havings.

INNER PEACE, CALM, AND STRENGTH

Know yourself, really!

"Knowing others is intelligence; knowing yourself is true wisdom." (Laozi, Tao Te Ching)

"Replace 'Why is this happening to me' with 'What is this trying to tell me'." (NN)

"Our background and circumstances influenced who we are, but we are responsible for who we become." (NN)

"You don't just wake up and become the butterfly – development is a process." (NN)

"It's not a matter of 'finding yourself' but rediscovering yourself under layers of judgement, doubt, and fear." (NN)

I think one of the best things I ever did in my life was start digging deep and asking myself Why am I the way I am? and Why do things the way I do? It takes a ton of work and intentionality, but getting to know yourself better will help you to live a life you really love.

Emotional Core Wounds from Childhood are deep-seated emotional injuries that often stem from early life experiences. These wounds can arise from unmet needs, neglect, criticism, abandonment, or other forms of emotional pain I encountered as a child. What I've come to understand is that these wounds usually remain unconscious, yet they profoundly shape how I see myself, how I behave, and how I relate to others as an adult.

They often show up as patterns of fear, insecurity, or self-sabotage, and they can result in me being easily triggered by certain situations. In trying to compensate for these wounds, I've noticed a tendency to pursue success obsessively, withdraw from others, or seek out relationships in an attempt to fill the void. Because these wounds were formed during a time when my emotional development was still in progress, they created limiting beliefs about myself and the world—beliefs like "I am not worthy" or "I am not lovable"

Healing these core wounds has involved recognizing and understanding them, often through self-reflection, therapy, or other healing practices, and working to rewrite the negative narratives they've instilled in me. I've found that addressing these wounds has been and is crucial for my personal growth, emotional wellbeing, and ability to form healthy, fulfilling relationships.

Inner Meaning

"The two most important days in your life are the day you are born and the day you find out why." (Mark Twain)

"Let yourself be silently drawn by the strange pull of what you really love. It will not lead you astray." (Rumi)

"Life is never made unbearable by circumstances, but only by lack of meaning and purpose." (Viktor Frankl)

"The inspiration you seek is already within you. Be silent and listen." (Rumi)

"Once a wise man was asked.... what is the meaning of life...? He replied..... Life itself has no meaning, Life is an opportunity to create a meaning..." (NN)

Society makes us believe that:

- We must have a purpose
- And it must be something big and earthshattering

But honestly, I no longer subscribe to this point of view. Why? Because most people assume that for instance doing good for others will bring them fulfillment. What many don't realize is that, deep down, we're often still seeking positive feedback, validation, recognition—or simply put: love. And that's okay—if we're aware of it.

I've come to the conclusion that real, lasting fulfillment doesn't necessarily come from grand, external purposes. Instead, it's more about adopting a mindset or attitude. For me, that means being willing to help others whenever I see a need. I'm not saying we shouldn't work for an NGO or fight global hunger, but do we even know our neighbors' names and offer help when they need it?

More importantly, I believe we first need to define what I call our "Inner Meaning"—the answer to "Why am I really here?" independent of the outside world, in non-material terms. Not in an egoistic way, but in an self-compassionate one.

What could this be? For me, it's about having inner peace, inner calm, and strength. Full stop. Only then can I handle life's challenges without getting triggered or emotionally thrown off course. From that place, I can live my outer purpose—a life rooted in compassion.

(Footnote: If you want to explore how to define your own Inner Meaning, check out the exercise section. It's simple, because deep down, we've always known it.)

BEING

How real is reality, really?

"Our real reality is beyond the five senses." (Deepak Chopra)

"Everything in existence is the same energy, manifesting itself in a million different ways." (Sadhguru)

"We are here to awaken from our Illusion of separateness." (Thich Nhat Hanh)

"The Being of Everything Is the Ocean of Oneness." (Rupert Spira)

"I dreamed I was a butterfly, flitting around in the sky; then I awoke. Now I wonder: Am I a man who dreamt of being a butterfly, or am I the butterfly dreaming that I am a man?" (Chuang Tzu)

Now, this is the most important part, in my humble opinion.

Most of us are constantly doing rather than simply being, feeling restless, depressed, bored or unhappy if we're not occupied. Caught up in the mind's habitual patterns—replaying the past or dreaming about the future—we struggle to live in the present moment.

This leads to a life driven by distractions, anxiety, and dissatisfaction, where even achieving our goals doesn't guarantee lasting happiness or, even less, true fulfillment.

But the "solution" is so simple and close that we usually overlook it:

I really like the English term "Human Being" We're all familiar with the "human" part, as we've discussed in the previous pages—our dreams, disappointments, fears, hopes, and expectations.

But what about the "being" part? In a world so focused on external achievements and roles, the concept of simply *being*—of nurturing the soul—is often overlooked.

For a long time, people believed the Earth was the center of the universe. Challenging that belief met with disbelief and resistance until it became accepted as truth.

Similarly, today's misconception is that our external world and our roles within it are the center of everything. That's what the ego and society constantly reinforce.

Questioning this belief naturally triggers resistance. But perhaps, just perhaps, we're at a point in human evolution where it's time to recognize that our internal world is just as important. Our soul and its growth deserve just as much attention.

It's time to rediscover the balance between *human* and *being*.

Spirituality, Non-Duality, and Quantum Mechanics

"There is oneness in existence and uniqueness in all beings. The essence of spirituality is to recognize and enjoy this." (Sadhguru)

"Quantum physics thus reveals a basic oneness of the universe." (Erwin Schrodinger)

"Attached to nothing, connected to everything." (NN)

"To offer no resistance to life is to be in a state of grace, ease, and lightness. This state is then no longer dependent upon things being in a certain way, good or bad. It seems almost paradoxical, yet when your inner dependency on form is gone, the general conditions of your life, the outer forms, tend to improve greatly." (Eckhart Tolle)

"How wonderful, how wonderful, everything is perfect, exactly the way it is." (Taoist Saying)

And here's the tough part (it took me ages to reach this point, and honestly, it's still an ongoing process):

I've come to realize that reality isn't what our limited five senses lead us to believe.

Let me put it this way: Imagine the ocean and two waves approaching the shore. One panics, shouting, "Oh no, we're going to crash, we're going to die!". The other wave calmly responds, "Don't be silly, you're part of the ocean—you can't die".

We're all like those waves, driven by our egos and fears. What we've forgotten is that we're also part of the ocean—something much bigger and deeper than our individual identities. When we allow ourselves to move beyond the limitations of being just the wave, we still remain ourselves, but we undergo a profound transformation.

Sure, we'll still carry some conditioning, as no one can be completely free of the influence from how we were raised or the environments we live in. But this conditioning no longer causes suffering. Even when faced with challenges—because challenges will continue to come as we grow—the difference is that now, these challenges can deepen our awareness. They make us more conscious, curious, and peaceful, gradually quieting the reactive and complaining mind.

Another beautiful effect is that we become less attached to expectations. We'll still give our best in any situation, guided by compassion, but our inner peace and harmony no longer depend on achieving success or meeting specific goals.

Being starts to merge into the human experience, and as a result, the conditioned self becomes less troublesome, less dysfunctional, and stops creating unnecessary suffering for ourselves and others.

You become fully present, fully at peace in the now.

You simply are.

Coming Home

"Who can make the muddy water clear? Let it be still and it will gradually become clear." (Laozi, Tao Te Ching)

"The wise man is one who knows what he does not know." (Laozi, Tao Te Ching)

"The journey of a thousand miles begins with a single step." (Laozi, Tao Te Ching)

"Here's a big secret about the mind: when you stop fighting, it becomes silent naturally." (NN)

"Manifest plainness, embrace simplicity, reduce selfishness, have few desires, practice compassion." (Laozi, Tao Te Ching)

At the end of the day, it all comes down to coming home—becoming aware of who I really am and what life, or so-called reality, truly is beyond the limits of our five senses.

What is my true, unchanging essence?

The roles I've played in life—child, student, husband, father, grandfather, keynote speaker, counselor—have always been in flux.

My experiences have varied greatly, filled with ups and downs.

Even my body is constantly changing, with all my cells completely replaced every few years. Physically, I'm not the same person I was years ago, neither in appearance nor in molecular structure.

The same applies to my thoughts and beliefs; they're not the same as they were 10, 25, or 50 years ago.

So, if we strip away everything that's constantly shifting in our lives, what remains as the unchanging essence, the "real me"?

Being.

To help my mind grasp this, I've given it a label: in my case, I call it the "ocean" Others might call it the Soul, Dao, Divine, the field of unlimited possibilities, consciousness—whatever resonates with you.

But that's it.

I am.

Nature

"Nature does not hurry, yet everything is accomplished." (Laozi, Tao Te Ching)

"Look deep into nature, and then you will understand everything better." (Albert Einstein)

"In the tip of every blade of grass, the entire universe is reflected." (Chuang Tse)

"A walk in nature walks the soul back home." (Mary Davis)

"I firmly believe that nature brings solace in all troubles." (Anne Frank)

Sometimes, you catch glimpses of this when you immerse yourself in nature. When you're fully present in nature, it can aid in the awakening. In those moments, when you become aware of awareness itself, it just happens.

Sometimes, it occurs almost by accident—while climbing a mountain or swimming in the wild—you suddenly feel the person you think you are recede, leaving only pure awareness. You might believe it's caused by the beauty you're seeing, but it's really about the quieting of thought. And this can even happen in the middle of a busy city.

This practice becomes an ongoing, effortless approach—being present without expecting any specific results.

Can you, in a relaxed way, simply become aware? Just observe and let go of habitual, especially self-serving thoughts—the kind that only reinforce the fictitious self, the ego, which thrives on its own problems.

It's not about fighting these thoughts, but rather observing—maybe even embracing them—and, in doing so, naturally letting them go. As the awakening deepens, the clouds begin to clear, and the sun, which has always been shining, starts to break through.

My Trick

"A good traveler has no fixed plans and is not intent on arriving." (Laozi, Tao Te Ching)

"Great undertakings are always achieved through small things." (I Ching)

"Humility is the foundation of all virtues." (I Ching)

"The quieter you become, the more you are able to hear." (Rumi)

"Between stimulus and response there is a space. In that space is our power to choose our response." (Viktor Frankl)

Throughout my life's journey, I've discovered a simple approach—or a "trick," if you will—that makes things easier, more fulfilling, and enjoyable for me (and hopefully for those around me). It's straightforward (I'm a fan of the KISS principle—Keep It Simple, Stupid), and it works for me:

I view life as a play, a movie, or a VR game where I'm simultaneously the actor, the director, and the audience.

When something "nice" happens, I dive fully into it and enjoy it.

When something "not so nice" happens? As I mentioned earlier, it's not what happens to us that causes suffering, but how we interpret it. So, I go fully into it as well, reminding myself: "It's not really real; it's just energy—I fully accept it and ask: what can I learn from it?"

And yes, you might call it a "trick," but it works for me.

Now, you have to find your own "trick".

Brush Your Soul: Give It the Care It Deserves

"We suffer more often in imagination than in reality." (Seneca)

"You have power over your mind—not outside events. Realize this, and you will find strength." (Marcus Aurelius)

"By letting go, it all gets done." (Laozi, Tao Te Ching)

"The wound is the place where the light enters you." (Rumi)

"Silence is essential. We need silence, just as much as we need air, just as much as plants need light. If our minds are crowded with words and thoughts, there is no space for us" (Thích Nhat Hanh)

Just like brushing your teeth is essential for your health, brushing your soul is vital for your well-being. Take time, even once a week, to nurture your inner self. Whether it's a slow, mindful walk in nature or indulging in creative activities like painting, writing, or playing music, or simply taking some moments to reflect on your life —make it a ritual to reconnect with yourself. Start small, but make it intentional. Your soul deserves as much care as your body.

Take a moment. Brush your soul.

That's it.

**EXERCISES
TO
GET TO KNOW YOURSELF
AND TO
LIVE A LIFE YOU TRULY LOVE**

As said before, I'm a big fan of the KISS principle (Keep It Simple, Stupid), inspired by something I learned from Paul Watzlawick: "Contrary to popular belief, complex problems require simple solutions"

Here are some simple – yet profound – exercises to help you to live a life you love:

Sources of Fulfillment

From Emotional Core Wounds To Emotional Core Gifts

Inner Meaning

More than a Gratitude Journal

Slowing Down, Slow Motion

The fastest way to freedom

Brushing Your Soul

Being

There are more deep exercises like

Voice Dialogue

And especially profound: Accessing your Inner Wisdom (You have all the answers inside yourself)

Feel free to let me know if you want some information or help with any of these exercise (dl@langenecker.com)

Reflecting on Sources of Fulfillment

Objective: To identify and differentiate between external sources of happiness and internal sources of fulfillment in your life.

Duration: Approximately 30 minutes

Materials Needed: Journal or paper, pen

Step 1: Find a Quiet Space

Choose a comfortable and quiet environment where you can reflect without interruptions.

Step 2: Reflect on External Achievements

1. **List External Milestones:** Write down 3-5 significant external achievements or acquisitions in your life. These could include promotions, awards, purchases, or any milestones you believed would bring happiness.

2. **Assess Their Impact:**

   - For each item, answer the following questions:

   - **Initial Feelings:** How did you feel immediately after achieving or acquiring it?

   - **Duration of Happiness:** How long did that feeling last?

   - **Long-Term Impact:** Did this achievement contribute to lasting fulfillment or was it a fleeting moment of joy?

Step 3: Reflect on Internal Experiences

1. **List Moments of Inner Contentment:** Write down 3-5 experiences where you felt deep inner satisfaction, contentment, or peace. These could involve personal growth, acts of kindness, moments of connection, or overcoming challenges.

2. **Assess Their Impact:**

   - For each experience, consider the following:

     - **Emotional Resonance:** How did this experience make you feel?

     - **Longevity:** Did the sense of fulfillment last longer compared to external achievements?

     - **Influence on Personal Growth:** How did this experience contribute to your personal development or worldview?

Step 4: Compare and Reflect

- **Analysis:** Look at both lists side by side. Reflect on the differences in how external achievements and internal experiences have impacted your sense of fulfillment.

- **Questions to Ponder:**

  - Which sources brought more lasting contentment?

  - How have these reflections shifted your perspective on pursuing happiness versus cultivating fulfillment?

Step 5: Set Intentions

Based on your reflections:

- **Identify Actions:** Write down 2-3 actionable steps you can take to prioritize internal sources of fulfillment in your daily life. Examples might include dedicating time to a passion project, practicing mindfulness, nurturing relationships, or engaging in community service.

- **Commitment:** Consider how you will integrate these actions into your routine. Set realistic and compassionate goals for yourself.

Remember: This exercise is a tool for self-discovery. There are no right or wrong answers. The goal is to gain clarity on what truly brings you lasting fulfillment and to encourage a shift towards nurturing those internal sources.

From Emotional Core Wounds To Core Gifts

Objective: To become aware of emotional wounds from childhood that still subconsciously affect you, and to work on aligning and harmonizing with them.

Duration: Approximately 30 minutes

Materials Needed: Journal or paper, pen

As someone who has done work on yourself, you are well aware that difficult life experiences can cause deep wounds to your psyche that can be hard to release.

Whether these came from significant childhood traumas like verbal or mental abuse or from less extreme experiences, the impact of these wounds continues to shape your experience of the world.

Most of us, when wounded, make significant unconscious commitments for how to navigate life so as to avoid a similar wound. Such choices — for example, about what you need to do (or not do) to receive love, how you show up with others, and whether you feel safe — contribute to deep mental and emotional patterns that drive your thoughts, feelings and actions to this day.

These patterns can have many negative consequences for your life, such as inhibiting your self expression and freedom, damaging your relationships, or blocking your ability to move forward on exciting opportunities.

If you're like most of us, you are aware of (at least some of) your wounds, their resulting patterns and the negative impacts they have and are consciously working to move beyond them. But...

You may not be seeing much change and have diminishing hope that you can ever actually transform your patterns and have the experience of life you imagine.

There are many therapies and methods you may have tried that help bring awareness to your wounds and give some catharsis around them, but these techniques often don't fundamentally transform your experience of the wound.

When all's said and done, the wound and the patterns are still driving the ship.

Just ask yourself: do you still fall into the same damaging behavior patterns when you're stressed or overwhelmed?

Or do you find yourself unable to pursue your life purpose and goals because of limiting beliefs, old behaviors, resistance and fears?

These are signs that your wounding is still running the show.

Until you are able to transform your relationship to your wound — you are destined to live at the mercy of your limiting patterns.

Step 1:

Identify the Emotional Wound(s)

What was the wound, as best as you understand it? If you're unsure, speculate! (Examples: parental criticism, comparisons with siblings, being ignored, losing a grandparent, living in a war zone, being bullied at school, experiencing a natural disaster, etc. If it's hard to recall, speculate what it might have been.)

Step 2:

Identify the Emotion

Close your eyes. Reflect on the experience and try to identify the emotion you felt at the time. Find words that describe the feeling (and if you're unsure, imagine what someone might feel in that situation). Focus on the emotional experience. (Examples: hatred, loneliness, feeling stupid, feeling invisible, etc.)

Step 3:

Uncover the Belief

What belief did you unconsciously create about yourself? (Example: "I'm not good enough")

Step 4:

Identify Your Response

What decision(s) did you make? What did you try to avoid, and what did you crave? What strategies did you develop as a result? (Examples: people-pleasing, striving for success, withdrawing, avoiding trust, etc.)

Step 5:

Recognize the Downside(s)

What have been the downsides of this strategy? (Examples: burnout, loneliness, difficulty forming lasting relationships, etc.)

Step 6:

Discover Your Core Gifts

What are the upsides of this strategy? What skills and abilities have you developed because of your Emotional Core Wounds? (Examples: independence, resilience, organizational skills, speaking multiple languages, being able to "read" people, etc.)

Conclusions and Takeaway:

Reflect on what you've learned from this exercise.

Inner Meaning

Objective: To gain awareness of your true purpose for being on this planet, in non-material terms, independent of the outside world.

Duration: Approximately 15 minutes

Materials Needed: Journal or paper, pen

Ask yourself this question:

One day, when you're lying on your deathbed, what feelings will allow you to say, "Yes, it has been a fulfilling life"?

(Examples: inner peace, harmony, compassion, a sense of oneness, etc.) Focus solely on what matters to you, not in an egotistical way, but in an egocentric way—centered on your true self.

Knowing your Inner Meaning will make it easier to define your Outer Purpose and to make decisions in life. For example, you can ask yourself, "Will path A or B help me fulfill my Inner Meaning?"

To access your inner wisdom, it may be helpful to take a walk in nature or relax in a hot bath. Allow yourself to listen to whatever arises from within.

More than a Gratitude Journal

Objective: To end your day not only on a positive note but also by giving yourself the love and recognition we often seek from others.

Duration: Approximately 1 minute

Materials Needed: Journal or paper, pen or penzu.com

Write down

3 Small Things I Experienced Today and I'm Grateful For:

(Include things we often take for granted, like health, having a roof over our heads, food on the table, etc.)

2 Small Things I Did Today and I Feel Good About

1 Thing I Would Do Differently if It Happened Again

At the end of each week, take a moment to reflect on your entries. Notice the positive and beautiful things in your life—things we often overlook due to the challenges in our daily routines.

Feel the positive energy rise within you as you realize how many beautiful and positive things are happening in your life. It's a reminder to not just focus on "the holes in the cheese, but to appreciate the cheese itself"

Slowing Down/"Slow Motion"

Objective: To practice mindfulness

Duration: ideally once a day

Materials Needed: none

Do routine tasks like brushing your teeth or washing the dishes in slow motion for about five minutes. Focus entirely on the task at hand. When your thoughts inevitably wander, gently bring your attention back to what you're doing, without judgment.

The Fastest Way to Freedom

Objective: Who are you in essence?

Duration: 5 minutes

Materials Needed: none, simply read the dialogue, and apply it to yourself afterwards

Simply read the following dialogue:

Participant: I have a question about freedom.

Facilitator: So, tell us about yourself.

Participant: There are many stories I could tell.

Facilitator: We're not looking for stories about things that have happened to you or things you've done. We want to know about you.

Participant: When you asked that, there was this gap, this lostness—I couldn't find it.

Facilitator: That's the direction to explore. Tell us more.

Participant: I was searching for the right question or answer.

Facilitator: Don't search for the right answer. Just tell us about yourself.

Participant: It's something in the heart that knows what the self is, but it's tricky—it knows and doesn't know at the same time. So when you ask, I go to the heart to find the answer.

Facilitator: Don't go to the heart; go to yourself. Don't go to your thoughts or anywhere else—just go to yourself.

Participant: I cannot answer.

Facilitator: That's a good sign. Why can't you answer?

Participant: Because it feels like any answer would betray what it actually is.

Facilitator: Exactly. Any answer would impose a limit on what you are, and you intuitively know that limit would be untrue.

Participant: It's like wearing different identities, like a t-shirt. Sometimes I wear the identity of a mother, but I know these roles aren't who I really am. I've struggled with these identities.

Facilitator: You're right—these identities are like t-shirts. You were yourself before you were a mother, so being a mother is not who you essentially are; it's just a role. But you're the link that connects all those identities. Whenever you say, "I am," it's you qualifying yourself. What's the unqualified self—what are you before you take on any identity, role, or experience?

Participant: It's like space—unlimited, unbound.

Facilitator: That's it. You've identified the fastest way to freedom. The space you speak of is not bound by anything, just as your true nature is inherently free. Freedom isn't something you become; it's what you already are. It's not about acquiring freedom through effort or practice; it's about recognizing what you've always been beneath all the layers of experience and identity.

Participant: I expected freedom to feel more like wild energy, but this spacious quality doesn't feel wild.

Facilitator: Freedom expresses itself differently in everyone. For some, it's wild energy; for others, it's peace or sensitivity. Don't dictate how freedom should appear. Let it remain free to show up in various forms in your experience.

And now do this exercise yourself: If you set aside all temporary factors—your age, the roles you play or have played in your life, your thoughts, feelings, and even your body's cells—what remains as your unchanging essence?

Brushing Your Soul, Silence

Objective: To find Your Inner Peace

Duration: flexible

Materials Needed: none

Most of us avoid silence because it forces us to confront ourselves, and what we often find staring back is a sense of emptiness. We might also fear silence because we associate it with insignificance. We long to be seen, heard, and validated by others, striving to feel relevant and "somebody" in the eyes of the world.

This desire to be noticed can be overwhelming, but in our quest for recognition, we often drown out the voice within us that holds the answers we seek. The truth is, we already have everything we need inside. The peace we chase isn't out there somewhere—it's right here, in this moment, within us.

If you want to truly know yourself, try this exercise:

1. **Disconnect from External Noise:** Turn off the TV, radio, internet, and quiet the constant chatter in your mind. Go to a place where you can be alone without distractions.

2. **Sit in Silence:** Spend time simply being with yourself in complete silence. Allow any discomfort or restlessness to surface without judgment—this is where you begin to meet your true self.

3. **Listen Deeply:** As you sit in silence, notice what arises within you. In the quiet, your inner voice becomes clearer. You may find that your desires simplify, and a sense of contentment begins to emerge. You realize that you're already everything you need to be.

4. **Make It a Routine:** Like brushing your teeth, exercising, or eating, dedicate time in your schedule for silence each day. This practice is more than just a break from the noise—it's where you find strength, clarity, and purpose that guide you in all your actions.

5. **Integrate Silence into Daily Life:** Cultivate this stillness regularly so that you can carry a sense of peace into your daily routine, even amidst stress and challenges.

Guard this time—it's vital for your well-being. Silence isn't empty; it's full of the insights and calm you need to navigate life with greater resilience and clarity.

Being

Objective: None

Duration: ongoing

Materials Needed: none

Just be in the now, with awareness, embracing whatever the moment brings

EPILOGUE

It all comes back to what the old mystics have always said: it's not about learning something new or acquiring more; it's about letting go.

One of the key lessons in the *Bhagavad Gita* is that it's possible to take action without getting lost in the desire for the outcome—what the *Gita* calls "the fruit of the action." It says, "Don't give excessive attention to the fruit of the action; just be conscious of the action itself." This is seen as a spiritual practice.

First, we need to let go of the myth that enlightenment is some glorious event we imagine it to be. Whatever you think the Great Awakening, enlightenment, or self-realization is, I invite you to set that idea aside—it's just a speculation of the mind.

Enlightenment isn't an experience; it's like the clouds parting to reveal the sun that's always been there. The mind, the ego, quiets down for a moment, and what's left is the real you that has always been present.

We practice compassion towards ourselves and others, cultivate the highest virtues, and focus on healing. Enlightenment isn't a reward for effort or good behavior; it's freely available to anyone, with no prerequisites.

This journey is about becoming a healthy, whole, loving human being, knowing that it won't be rewarded by anything external. You do everything you can, and at some point, you realize it's no longer in your control.

Even as you engage in inner work or self-development, you know deep down it's not about the reward—it's simply the best way to live a human life. Your heart remains open and surrendered to that which is beyond what we can achieve—whether you call it Grace, the touch of Truth, or the Invisible Hand of Love.

There's a profound sense of surrender and humility in recognizing that you can't "do" it, and that this recognition is the only thing that truly matters.

Let go of any idea that you know what it is, and just be with yourself—empty of everything that isn't truly you. That's the deepest practice you can engage in.

For the first time in lifetimes, you're not chasing an experience—you're simply being yourself.

You allow unconditioned consciousness to act through you, fully present in the moment, giving your undivided attention to whatever you're doing right now.

And then, you have a foot in both worlds.

Because You are more than you think you are

When you recognize that, you see what a gift it truly is.

I hope this is helpful to you.

Following you can find some more quotes that have helped me along my journey; maybe some of them will be helpful for you too.

And feel free to get in touch with me for any question you might have: dl@langenecker.com

INSPIRING QUOTES

"May such calm of soul be mine, so as to meet the force of circumstances." (Aeschylus)

"The obstacle is the way." (Marcus Aurelius, Meditations)

"It is not death that a man should fear, but he should fear never beginning to live." (Marcus Aurelius, Meditations)

"He who fears death will never do anything worth of a man who is alive." (Seneca)

"Before the beginning of great brilliance, there must be chaos." (I Ching*)

"When a thing is due to happen, nothing can stop it; if it is not due, it will not happen." (I Ching)

"Waste no more time arguing what a good man should be. Be one." (Marcus Aurelius, Meditations)

"If it is not right, do not do it; if it is not true, do not say it." Marcus Aurelius, Meditations)

"The happiness of your life depends upon the quality of your thoughts." (Marcus Aurelius, Meditations)

"It is not events that disturb people, it is their judgments concerning them." (Epictetus, Enchiridion)

"He who laughs at himself never runs out of things to laugh at." (Epictetus)

"Don't explain your philosophy. Embody it." (Epictetus)

"Wealth consists not in having great possessions, but in having few wants." (Epictetus)

"Difficulty shows what men are." (Epictetus)

"Luck is what happens when preparation meets opportunity." (Seneca)

"The sage does not hoard. The more he helps others, the more he benefits himself." (I Ching)

"He who can meet the demands of the time is wise." (I Ching)

"Creativity comes from awakening and directing men's higher natures, which originate in the spiritual realms." (I Ching)

"He who deliberates fully before taking a step will spend his entire life on one leg." (I Ching)

"He who overcomes himself is mighty." (I Ching)

"Don't grieve. Anything you lose comes round in another form." (Rumi)

"Silence is a source of great strength." (Laozi, Tao Te Ching)

"Yesterday I was clever, so I wanted to change the world. Today I am wise, so I am changing myself." (Rumi)

"What you seek is seeking you." (Rumi)

"Your task is not to seek for love, but merely to seek and find all the barriers within yourself that you have built against it." (Rumi)

"The soul has been given its own ears to hear things the mind does not understand." (Rumi)

"You were born with wings, why prefer to crawl through life?" (Rumi)

"Those who have a 'why' to live, can bear with almost any 'how'." (Viktor Frankl)

"In some ways suffering ceases to be suffering at the moment it finds a meaning." (Viktor Frankl)

"Forces beyond your control can take away everything you possess except one thing, your freedom to choose how you will respond to the situation." (Viktor Frankl)

"The salvation of man is through love and in love." (Viktor Frankl)

"Life is never made unbearable by circumstances, but only by lack of meaning and purpose." (Viktor Frankl)

"Flow with whatever may happen, and let your mind be free: Stay centered by embracing whatever you are doing. This is the ultimate." (Chuang Tzu)

"He who knows that enough is enough will always have enough." (Chuang Tzu)

"The perfect man employs his mind as a mirror. It grasps nothing; it refuses nothing. It receives but does not keep." (Chuang Tzu)

"The wise man looks into space and does not regard the small as too little, nor the great as too much; for he knows that there is no limit to dimension." (Chuang Tzu)

"To a mind that is still, the whole universe surrenders." (Chuang Tzu)

"The more you identify with your mind, the further away you are from your self." (Sadhguru)

"Stop waiting for Friday, for summer, for someone to fall in love with, for life. Fulfillment happens when you stop waiting and make the most of the moment you are in now." (NN)

"I am enough." (NN)

"May you never overlook how powerful it can be to slow down for a moment and take a little time to breathe." (Morgan Harper Nichols)

"We don't see things as they are, we see them as we are." (Anais Nin)

"And you can also commit injustice by doing nothing." (Marcus Aurelius)

"There is only one way to happiness and that is to cease worrying about things which are beyond the power of our will." (Epictetus)

"You want to know the difference between a master and a beginner? The master has failed more times than the beginner has ever tried." (Yoda)

"Men for the sake of getting a living forget to live." (Margaret Fuller)

"Be the reason someone believes in the goodness of people." (NN)

"That which you most need will be found where you least to look." (CG Jung)

"Work hard on yourself, but don't be hard on yourself." (JP Crimi)

"I'm so at peace … I don't even want any revenge. You won. Just leave me alone." (NN)

"Freedom is not achieved by satisfying desire, but by eliminating it." (Epictetus)

"The soul becomes dyed with the color of its thoughts." (Marcus Aurelius)

"True Happiness is to enjoy the present, without anxious dependence upon the future." (Seneca)

"Every man takes the limits of his own field of vision for the limits of the world." (Arthur Schopenhauer)

"Sometimes being alone is the upgrade." (NN)

"You are allowed to outgrow people. This includes past versions of yourself." (Mandy Hale")

"Nothing gives you more joy than when your heart grows wider and wider and your sense of belonging to the universe grows deeper and deeper." (Br. David Steindl-Rast)

"Everyone thinks of changing the world, but no one of changing himself." (Leo Tolstoy)

"New opinions are always suspected, and usually opposed, without any other reason but because they are not common." (John Locke)

"No greater gift there is, than a generous heart." (Yoda)

"In the midst of movement and chaos, keep still inside you." (Deepak Chopra)

"Be happy for this moment. This moment is your life." (Omar Khayyam)

"There is nothing either good or bad, but thinking makes it so." (William Shakespeare)

"Begin at once to live, and count each separate day as a separate life." (Seneca)

"This is the secret of life: to be non-serious but absolutely involved." (Sadhguru)

"You should sit in meditation for 20 minutes a day. Unless you're too busy, then you should sit for an hour." (Zen Saying)

"Listen to the sound of silence." (Paul Simon)

"Simplicity is the ultimate sophistication." (Clare Boothe Luce)

"We delight in the beauty of a butterfly, but rarely admit the changes it has to go through to achieve that." (Maya Angelou)

"How much time do you give every day to your thoughts? How much time do you give every day to your inner silence?" (JC Dumont)

"Within you there is a stillness and a sanctuary to which you can retreat at any time and be yourself." (Hermann Hesse)

"You don't have to learn how to love yourself. You just have to remember there was nothing wrong with you to begin with. You just have to come home." (Nayyirah Waheed)

"Talk to yourself like you would talk to someone you love." (Brene Brown)

"I'm beginning to suspect that the second half of life is about learning to let go of everything I feverishly collected over the first half that wasn't loving or human." (Michael Xavier)

"The mind is like water. When it's turbulent, it's difficult to see. When it is calm, everything becomes clear." (NN)

"This place is a dream. Only a sleeper considers it real. The death comes like dawn, and you wake up laughing at what you thought was your grief." (Rumi)

"Faith is not about everything turning out okay. Faith is about being ok no matter how things turn out." (NN)

"Everyone you meet has something to teach you." (NN)

"What a wonderful life I've had! I only wish I'd realized it sooner." (Sidonie-Gabrielle Collette)

"May you grow still enough to hear the small noises earth makes in preparing for the long sleep of winter, so that you yourself may grow calm and grounded within." (BR. David Steindl-Rast)

"Let go of who you think you're supposed to be; embrace who you are." (Brene Brown)

"Do you need more knowledge? Is more information going to save the world, or faster computers, more scientific or intellectual analysis? Isn't it wisdom that humanity needs most at this time?." (Eckhart Tolle)

"Whoever is delighted in solitude is either a wild beast or a god." (Aristotele)

"The more we value things outside our control, the less control we have." (Epictetus)

"Life can only be understood backwards, but it must be lived forwards." (Soren Kierkegaard)

"Problems are solved not by giving new information but by arranging what we have known for long." (Ludwig Wittgenstein)

"We suffer more often in imagination than in reality." (Seneca)

"All of humanity's problems stem from man's inability to sit quietly in a room alone." (Blaise Pascal)

"If you could kick the person in the pants responsible for most of your trouble, you wouldn't be able to sit for a month." (Theodore Roosevelt)

"Everything in the way is part of the way." (Guy Finley)

"I may not have gone where I intended to go, bit I think I have ended up where I needed to be." (Douglas Adams)

"The wise man is one who knows what he does not know." (Laozi, Tao Te Ching)

"Manifest plainness, embrace simplicity, reduce selfishness, have few desires." (Laozi, Tao Te Ching)

"Waste no more time arguing what a good man should be. Be one." (Marcus Aurelius, Meditations)

"Your assumptions are your windows on the world. Scrub them off every once in a while, or the light won't come in." (Isaak Asimov)

"Expectations are the greatest impediment to living. In anticipation of tomorrow, we lose today." (Seneca)

"Expect nothing. Appreciate everything." (NN)

"Maybe they will choose you … maybe they won't. But none of it matters if you choose yourself." (NN)

"A path is made by walking on it." (Zhuang Zhou)

"Sometimes you just need to relax and trust that things will work out. Let go a little and let life happen." (NN)

"Train yourself to let go of everything you fear to lose." (Yoda)

"Owning our story can be hard but not nearly as difficult as spending our lives running from it. Embracing our vulnerabilities is risky but not nearly as dangerous as giving up on love and belonging and joy - the experiences that make us the most vulnerable. Only when we are brave enough to explore the darkness will we discover the infinite power of our light." (Brené Brown)

"The quieter you become, the more you are able to hear." (Rumi)

"There is more to life than increasing its speed." (Mahatma Gandhi)

"Sometimes the most important thing in a whole day is the rest we take between two deep breaths." (Etty Hillesum)

"The quality of human life will only truly change when we change within ourselves." (Sadhguru)

"You don't get to choose how you're going to die. Or when. You can only decide how you're going to live. Now." (Joan Baez)

"Every day the world will drag you by the hand yelling 'This is important! And this is important', 'You need to worry about this! And this!' And each day, it's up to you to yank your hand back, put it on your heart and say, 'No, this is important!' " (Ian Thomas)

"If you want to awaken all of humanity, then awaken all of yourself, if you want to eliminate the suffering in the world, then eliminate all that is dark and negative in yourself. Truly, the greatest gift you have to give is that of your own self-transformation." (Lao Tzu)

"The rush and pressure of modern life are a form, perhaps the most common form, of its innate violence. To allow oneself to be carried away by a multitude of conflicting concerns, to surrender to too many demands, to commit oneself to too many projects, to want to help everyone in everything, is to succumb to violence. The frenzy of our activity neutralizes our work for peace. It destroys our own inner capacity for peace. It destroys the fruitfulness of our own work, because it kills the root of inner wisdom which makes work fruitful." (Thomas Merton)

"Real love is always chaotic. You lose control; you lose perspective. You lose the ability to protect yourself. The greater the love, the greater the chaos. It's a given and that's the secret." (Jonathan Carroll, White Apples)

"I used to want to find someone who checked all the boxes on my list. Boy, did I have it all wrong. Now I see love and relationships are about finding someone who not only vibes with you, but also wants to continue to grow and evolve as a person. Relationships are an invitation to be our best selves and a container to do just that. If they're not calling you out, they're not the one. Being powerful doesn't scare great partners, it attracts them, it turns them on, it gives them soulgasms." (Mark Groves)

"Don't hope that events will turn out the way you want, welcome events in whichever way they happen, this is the path to peace." (Marcus Aurelius)

"If we take eternity to mean not infinite temporal duration but timelessness, then eternal life belongs to those who live in the present." (Ludwig Wittgenstein)

"To offer no resistance to life is to be in a state of grace, ease, and lightness. This state is then no longer dependent upon things being in a certain way, good or bad. It seems almost paradoxical, yet when your inner dependency on form is gone, the general conditions of your life, the outer forms, tend to improve greatly." (Eckhart Tolle)

"Be thankful for those that are tuned into your frequency. They are your reminders that on the deepest level of our existence, we are one." (NN)

"If you would be a real seeker after truth, it is necessary that at least once in your life you doubt, as far as possible, all things." (René Descartes)

"There is no good or bad without us, there is only perception. There is the event itself and the story we tell ourselves about what it means." (Ryan Holiday)

"The capacity to be alone is the capacity to love." (NN)

"It may look paradoxical to you, but it's not. It is an existential truth: only those people who are capable of being alone are capable of love, of sharing, of going into the deepest core of another person--without possessing the other, without becoming dependent on the other, without reducing the other to a thing, and without becoming addicted to the other.

They allow the other absolute freedom, because they know that if the other leaves, they will be as happy as they are now. Their happiness cannot be taken by the other, because it is not given by the other." (Osho)

"If you have a hard time setting healthy boundaries, always remember this: people who love you and truly care about you want you to love and respect yourself. People who only care about what you do for them are the ones who will have issues with your boundaries." (Sylvester Mcnutt III)

"I'm slowly learning that even if I react, it won't change anything, it won't make people suddenly love and respect me, it won't magically change their minds.

Sometimes it's better to just let things be, let people go, don't fight for closure, don't ask for explanations, don't chase answers and don't expect people to understand where you're coming from. I'm slowly learning that life is better lived when you don't center it on what's happening around you and center it on what's happening inside you instead. Work on yourself and your inner peace." (NN)

"You are responsible for your happiness.

In fact, you create it. You attract it. You manifest it. You are the architect of your reality. You choose your thoughts, your perceptions, and your reaction to external forces.

You possess all of the tools needed to expand your awareness, to orchestrate the evolution of your consciousness, to choose happiness, to choose love. You are that powerful.

Create the life you deserve. Vibrate love." (NN)

"Existence is one whole process. You are not a separate entity." (Sadhguru)

"Open your eyes to the beauty around you, open your mind to the wonders of life, open your heart to those who love you, and always be true to yourself." (Maya Angelou)

"Happiness is a choice, not a result. Nothing will make you happy until you choose to be happy. No person will make you happy unless you decide to be happy. Your happiness will not come to you. It can only come from you." (NN)

"In an age of speed, I began to think, nothing could be more invigorating than going slow. In an age of distraction, nothing can feel more luxurious than paying attention. And in an age of constant movement, nothing is more urgent than sitting still." (Pico Iyer)

"Somebody said something to you that is rude or designed to hurt?

Instead of going into unconscious reaction or negativity, such as attack, defense or withdrawal, you let it pass right through you. Offer no resistance. It is as if there's nobody there to get hurt anymore.

That is forgiveness. In this way, you become invulnerable." (Eckhart Tolle)

"When you arise in the morning, think of what a precious privilege it is to be alive - to breathe, to think, to enjoy, to love." (Marcus Aurelius)

"Signs of maturity:

1. Small talks no longer excite you.

2. Sleep is better than a Friday night out.

3. You forgive more.

4. You become more open-minded.

5. You respect differences.

6. You don't force love.

7. You accept heartaches.

8. You don't judge easily.

9. You sometimes prefer to be silent than to engage in a nonsense fight.

10. Your happiness doesn't depend on people but on your inner self." (NN)

"One small act of kindness each day, for myself and for others, is enough to create a day full of fulfillment and joy." (NN)

"A journey of a thousand miles begins with a single step." (Lao Tzu)

And here is my favorite poem:

"Desiderata

Go placidly amid the noise and haste,
and remember what peace there may be in silence.

As far as possible without surrender

be on good terms with all persons.
Speak your truth quietly and clearly;
and listen to others,
even to the dull and the ignorant;
they too have their story.

Avoid loud and aggressive persons,
they are vexatious to the spirit.
If you compare yourself with others,
you may become vain or bitter,
for always there will be greater and lesser persons than yourself.
Enjoy your achievements as well as your plans.

Keep interested in your own career, however humble;
it is a real possession in the changing fortunes of time.

Exercise caution in your business affairs,
for the world is full of trickery.

But let this not blind you to what virtue there is;
many persons strive for high ideals,
and everywhere life is full of heroism.

Be yourself.
Especially, do not feign affection.
Neither be cynical about love,
for in the face of all aridity and disenchantment
it is as perennial as the grass.
Take kindly the counsel of the years,
gracefully surrendering the things of youth.
Nurture strength of spirit to shield you in sudden misfortune.
But do not distress yourself with dark imaginings.
Many fears are born of fatigue and loneliness.
Beyond a wholesome discipline,
be gentle with yourself.

You are a child of the universe
no less than the trees and the stars;
you have a right to be here.

And whether or not it is clear to you,

no doubt the universe is unfolding as it should.

Therefore be at peace with God,

whatever you conceive Him to be.

And whatever your labors and aspirations,

in the noisy confusion of life, keep peace with your soul.

With all its sham, drudgery, and broken dreams,

it is still a beautiful world.

Be cheerful.

Strive to be happy."

(Max Ehrmann)

ABOUT DIETER LANGENECKER

On a personal note, I was born in 1954 and am a father and grandfather.

I work with individuals who are looking to transition from success to fulfillment, from knowledge to wisdom, and from aging to sage-ing. My clients are those who:

- Sense that there must be more to life and seek to live with greater meaning
- Have achieved a more or less good life but are now facing a challenging period and see this as an opportunity for transformation
- Feel a deep calling to make a positive impact in the world

Ever since I met Viktor Frankl in the 1970s, my mission has been to help people live a fulfilling life based on meaning, wisdom, and inner peace—and to contribute to making the world a better place.

It's about having a partner who helps you access your inner wisdom and clarity, recognize where you might be holding yourself back, and support you in living a life you truly love.

Watch the short video at

www.langenecker.com/aboutme,

visit

www.langenecker.com

and

www.linkedin.com/groups/1920759

for more information,

and feel free to contact me with any questions you may have
(dl@langenecker.com)

Made in the USA
Columbia, SC
22 January 2025